I0107938

NETWORTHING

HOW TO DEVELOP A GROWTH MINDSET

DR. RACQUEL PALMER

CONTENTS

© Copyright 2020 - All rights reserved.

It is not legal to reproduce, duplicate, or transmit any part of this document in either electronic means or in printed format. Recording of this publication is strictly prohibited and any storage of this document is not allowed unless with written permission from the publisher except for the use of brief quotations in a book review.

ISBN: 978-1-7351919-0-4

DEDICATION

This book is dedicated to my social media brothers and sisters, who often share their struggles with me, seeking advice on how to move forward in achieving their goals. I must admit, while I am no perfectionist, I feel compelled to share with you tips that I have used to develop and maintain a growth mindset.
To my son King, my harshest yet most honest critic, Darrington, my deceased mom, and my dad, you have enriched my life in the humblest way, so I dedicate this book to you all.

INTRODUCTION

Everyone who knows me will tell you I'm an outgoing, fun person who enjoys a good party and loves traveling to different places. I am also a lover of food, so on any given weekend, when I'm not working, you can find me at one of those fine restaurants, either on a date night or with my son King. I'm just always on the go, looking for new, fun things to do because I'm a lover of life.

As a result of my outgoing persona, many are challenged as to how I am always up and about, but still manage to excel professionally and academically. The most common question I get from family and friends, especially on social media, is, "How do you get so much done but still find time to go out and enjoy yourself?"

For the most part, I always laugh and tell them just to stay focused. But, over time, I noticed this question was dominant in my Instagram DM and my Facebook inbox. It has even got to the point where friends have started asking me to have one-on-one consultations with them. It was at this point I realized that this was a real opportunity, and I needed to help not only my friends but everyone whom I can reach. So I decided to write this book to share my little secrets on how to develop and maintain a growth mindset in order to achieve your goals and boost your "NETWORTH."

"The secret of success is learning how to use pain and pleasure instead of having pain and pleasure use you. If you do that, you're in control of your life, but if you don't, your life will control you."

– Tony Robbins

PART I

LET YOUR PAST LIFE TAKE YOU CLOSER TO
YOUR LIFE GOALS

CHAPTER ONE: WHO AM I?

I am from a small community in Portland, Jamaica, called Breast Works. It is very small and intimate, and most people are blood-related, so for the most part, we live as a big family.

The crime rate was very low. We never had a shooting incident or anything of that nature, and we often slept with our doors open. My parents operated a small shop along with a "gambling house." But ironically, I could not take part in any of those games or have a drink if it was not soda or juice. I often operated the shop; hence my love for mathematics developed. My dad is known as "Tearup," the party animal, and my mom, "Mama P," because of her love for the Honorable Portia Simpson Miller. My mom was very strict and often said I would act and remain a child until I was of age. She was very intelligent and taught me Spanish at home even before I started it in school. She would check my books every day after school and never missed a parent-teacher meeting. She knew all my teachers, all my friends, and my friends' parents. She ensured we were always in line and counseled all my friends like they were hers. My mother was

3

a strong-willed person who stood up for what she believed in. She taught me from a very early age to fight for my beliefs and never let anyone bully me into thinking I wasn't capable of achieving anything. I can safely say, "Mommy built the fighter spirit within me."

Even though my mother and father were great parents, I wasn't always a good kid. There were certain subjects I liked in high school, some I hated, so I would often skip classes to hang out on what we called the "lazy bench" at the great Titchfield High School. When CXC results came out, I only received a total of four subjects. My mother was upset. She asked what I wanted to do, and I told her the subjects I wanted to sit, and she paid for them. I was successful in all the sittings making a total of eight subjects.

I began working numerous jobs, including at the Bank of Nova Scotia and the College of Agriculture, because my parents could not afford to send me to university. But, I just felt like something was missing, I wanted to get a degree because I liked teaching and law, and I knew that in order to excel in those fields, I needed a formal education.

With my first paycheck from the Bank of Nova Scotia, I paid to begin an Associate Degree in Business Studies at the Jamaica Institute of Management. Even though this was not my first choice of study, it was what I could afford at the time. That did not last long because my work hours were not conducive to school. I then told mom I wanted to become a police officer. She said, "Hell, no!" But, even though she kept trying to talk me out of it, I was determined, so I went to my dad, and he gave me the money to go to the Area 2 Police Headquarters, where I sat the police entrance exam. Daddy said, "I support you in anything you choose."

Upon sitting the police entrance exam, I scored the highest in my class but was later told I was disqualified because I was too short. Feeling disappointed and frustrated,

I held my head down and was walking out. An inspector saw me and asked what was wrong, and I told him. He asked what my qualifications were, and I told him eight CXCs. He said, go back inside and tell them that I am giving you an educational waiver. I began praying, and when I went back in, I was accepted. That same day I was given an assessment and an interview, and I was successful. I called mom and told her the exciting news, but she said, "Good for you, you on your own." Honestly, I only told her out of respect because I knew that I wanted to be a police officer, and nothing was going to stop me.

Two months later, I officially received the call for training, and a list was given to me. I took the list to mommy, and she purchased everything and said, "I trained you to be a leader, and I'm impressed, not even me could deter you from your dreams." That is where it all started. A few months later, I was officially a Police Officer in the Jamaica Constabulary Force.

To reach your goals, you must define them. That means understanding who you are and who you want to be. I knew for sure I wanted to impact people's lives positively. I also know that I have a strong personality, so to combine both, I knew being a Police Officer would be the perfect career choice for me. For many, defining their goals involves considerable self-reflection. Most people fall into a pattern of accepting the jobs or roles that come to them most easily. That might mean accepting the jobs they get through people they know. It may consist of following a path that is expected of them for one reason or another. In some cases, it might even mean managing the tasks that no one else wants to do. For the lucky, these types of inertia-driven paths can lead to fulfilling lives and careers. Many others, however, become overburdened with roles that they do not really enjoy and end up feeling stuck. Don't let that be you!!

How do you escape from roles and responsibilities that are starting to feel like chores, and learn to live your best life? Richard Nelson Bolles, author of the best-selling self-help book "What Color is Your Parachute," says the answer starts with love.

In an article Bolles wrote titled, "Why Pursuing Your Dreams is Still Important," he offered the following advice: "The word **Love** is important. You want to look for your passions (*what you'd most love to do*), rather than your competencies (*what you can do*)" Bolles is not the first one to tell people to use their heart to find the path to living a more fulfilling life. In fact, this message was taught thousands of years ago. As proof of this, look no further than the quote, "Choose a job you love, and you will never have to work a day in your life," which is widely attributed to Confucius, who lived from 551 BC to 479 BC.

The Confucian philosophy of using your heart to chart your path through life is ancient, but it is also modern. I am a living testimony of this. The idea of working as a bank teller, particularly coming from a small community with people who barely completed high school, seemed like the best thing since sliced bread. But was it the best choice for me? No, because my heart was not into it, I was only doing it for a check, and prosperity is not simply about finding success, it is about finding fulfillment. The two must go hand in hand.

So how does anyone begin to figure out the answer to the question, "Who am I?" What do you need to understand about yourself to move forward and attain your goals?

In the introduction to her book, "YouMap: Find Yourself, Blaze Your Path, Show the World!" author Kristin A. Sherry told the story of a woman she called "Lena" who had a job she hated, and a boss who had been trying to get rid of her. Sherry met Lena after Lena left a psychiatric ward following a breakdown due to stress. Sherry reviewed Lena's

StrengthsFinder results with her, and they both realized that none of Lena's talents were being used in her current job. Lena had been burdened by stress because she felt like she was a total failure. Upon learning that she wasn't a failure, just a misfit in her current job, Lena cried, and she told Sherry that she had hope for her future for the first time in months.

What is even more amazing is that when Sherry posted a short description of Lena's situation on LinkedIn, within days, the post had more than a million views and more than a thousand comments. Many of the comments were from people who also felt that they were "Lenas." They had held jobs where they didn't fit in or even friendships and relationships that made them feel like they had no value. It was only when they realized that they were not worthless, just miscast, that they were able to get themselves out of bad situations and move forward.

Lena was an extreme example. She was so horribly miscast that it affected her mental health. Many, many more of us are able to perform adequately in a role, even if we are not fulfilled. I was a good receptionist at the College of Agriculture, and a great teller at the Bank of Nova Scotia. But, I was only surviving; I was not thriving. In these types of situations, we can get so tied up in our obligations that we may never realize we might be better suited for something else. We may never take the time to ask ourselves who we are. We just endure, not realizing that there are better, more fulfilling paths for us that will lead to much greater happiness.

How does anyone begin to understand what their strengths are? What prompts most people to consider whether they are really happy? If they are at a point where they are questioning their happiness, how do they find their strengths? In short, how do people answer the question, "Who am I?"

There are many strategies that one may utilize to find inner strength. For myself, I wrote in a journal. I went through my likes and dislikes and what I would want to achieve in both the short term and long term. It is imperative that one sets realistic goals, so setting short-term goals is a very strategic method for obtaining your long-term goals. Reading is also essential because things change over time, so it is important to stay up to date.

In Lena's case, however, Sherry had used StrengthFinder, a tool from Gallup, Inc., (StrengthFinder has been rebranded as CliftonStrengths) to show Lena where her strengths lie. The tool was originally developed by psychologist Donald Clifton. He believed that psychology often studies what is wrong with people, rather than what is right about them and what would help them succeed. The theory behind Clifton's tool, according to Gallup, is that to turn your talents into strengths, you must identify them and nourish them.

CliftonStrengths identifies thirty-four attributes and divides them into four categories: strategic thinking, relationship building, influencing, and executing. Examples of the thirty-four attributes that CliftonStrengths identifies include relator, learner, intellection, achiever, deliberative, maximizer, and significance. People with the "relator" attribute for example, which falls within the relationship-building category, tend to build strong relationships that hold teams together. People with a dominant "significance" attribute, which falls within the influencing category, are people who want to be heard. They are people who speak up, but they may also be people who take charge and make sure others are heard. People with a strong "intellection" attribute, which falls within the strategic thinking category, are people who like mental activity and like to think. They like to absorb and analyze information that may inform better decisions.

Of course, very often, people don't have just one dominant attribute. I, for instance, fall within the relator and dominant significance realm. I am a big team player, but I have no issue taking on any leadership role. Some people possess a complicated web of dominant attributes that influence how they process information and how they interact with people. Proponents of CliftonSpeaks argue that understanding this web of attributes that makes up individual personalities helps people better answer the question of "Who Am I?" This type of analysis also helps individuals understand their strengths, their weaknesses, and what traits will help them ultimately succeed.

CliftonStrengths is not the only psychological tool used to help understand what attributes help people succeed. Wonderlic is perhaps best known for its quick IQ tests that grew in popularity in the 1940s and 1950s as a tool to help companies better assess candidates. Beginning in the 1990s, Wonderlic started expanding from its original IQ score to offer additional assessments that can help paint a more detailed picture of an individual's strengths. Wonderlic's WonScore includes an IQ test, as well as a motivation assessment, and a personality test that evaluates candidates on dependability, stress tolerance, open-mindedness, cooperation, and sociability. The point is that these broader measures are being offered because even employers are starting to realize that having happy, successful employees is not only about understanding what your employees know, it's about understanding who they are, and what personality strengths they will bring to work with them.

How do you learn to understand yourself without paying for an assessment test?

Bolles, the author of "What Color is Your Parachute," argues that part of the path to success and happiness involves avoiding preconceived definitions of who you are. Instead, you should define yourself by what motivates you. In an article titled, "The Secret to Keeping Hope Alive," Bolles states that some people define themselves by their job, or their field, or the company where they work. More successful people, however, don't define themselves by their jobs, but by their skills. Instead of their field, they talk about their interests. They don't just look for job openings; they consider what they ideally want to do. Hence, the reason I decided to re-evaluate myself and choose a more fulfilling and comfortable career in law enforcement. I love law, I have a strong personality, good leadership skills, and love helping people, so I knew law enforcement would be my ideal match because it incorporates everything I love doing. That is what I feel would make me comfortable. But don't be fooled. If, after I got here, it wasn't what I perceived it to be, I would have re-evaluated myself and moved on because it is imperative that I find my purpose and a meaningful career in order to build my "networth."

Defining yourself is also very crucial in being successful. Instead of thinking of yourself as an engineer, you might want to think of yourself as a puzzle-solver, who likes to analyze. Maybe instead of thinking of yourself as a teacher, you might describe yourself as someone who wants to help people, and as someone who is outgoing and comfortable speaking to a crowd. I think of myself as a "jack of all trades." As a police officer, I wear many hats because people look to us to solve all the problems even when we are not specialists in the field. So, I'm not just a police officer preventing and detecting crime. I am a mom, a teacher, a counselor, a problem-solver, a public speaker, a nurse. I am many things, and I can do all of them well, so I can survive in many other positions other than being a police officer. There are no limits as to what I can achieve. This is important because defining yourself by merely what your job description says can be limiting. You don't just teach, you *are*, and you can do much more. So, define yourself by what you like, what you want, who you are, rather than just what you do. This can open up many new possibilities. You may find joy and inspiration in other things beyond what you currently do, whether that means finding a new job, or whether that just means taking on new projects, like volunteering, or pursuing your hobbies. Defining yourself in a way that keeps you open to new possibilities is likely to lead to a positive, optimistic outlook because there are so many other experiences you may encounter that you never expected. This open-mindedness is very significant to not only be successful but also to be happy.

CHAPTER TWO: PROGRAM YOUR MIND TO BE POSITIVE, EVEN IN A NEGATIVE SITUATION

E veryone encounters negativity at some point in their lives. However, it is crucial not to dwell on any form of negativity. You must train your mind to be positive even in a negative situation.

On December 30, 2013, I went through the most painful day of my entire life. That was the day I received a devastating phone call telling me that my mother had passed away. Let's be frank, I saw death coming, I knew she was going to die because she was ailing for some time, but I thought I had it all planned out. I knew it was going to break me a little because we were extremely close. I was her only child. She called me twenty times per day. She always had my back, She fought all my battles, so I knew I was going to be deeply wounded for a while. But, I honestly never expected it to wound me so deeply because I actually saw her death creeping up and thought I had it all planned out. Little did I know that death is something no one can prepare for. The day I received that phone call, my heart was shattered in pieces. Where was the plan I had in place all this time? All that went out of the window.

When mom passed, I had recently migrated to the United States. So I had to start planning her burial in Jamaica from overseas. On the day of the funeral, I did not cry. Many wondered about this, but I was so crippled inside that my tears were dry. A few days later, I boarded a plane back to the United States. Throughout my flight, I had many questions. I was to begin school for my master's degree in five days. I began questioning myself as to whether I could do this because I was in so much pain. I decided to reach out to my school counselor and told him about the situation. He told me not to begin classes because I wouldn't be focused, and my grades would be bad. He deferred my acceptance to the next quarter, which would be September 2014. But for some strange reason, this did not sit well with my soul.

Two days before the start of school, I went down on my knees, and I prayed, and I cried. I spoke to God in a language only he understands. Whilst on my knees, I called my school counselor, and I said, "No, I'm not deferring until the next quarter. I want to start school now." He asked if I was sure and I told him yes, I would handle it, I would do it. I boldly took this step because my mother taught me to be a fighter, and putting off school to mourn her death seemed like I was giving up on my dreams, and she definitely would not want this.

He said, "Ok, just remember, I'm here to help you the best way I can." I said ok and thanked him but told him the best way to help me right then was to ensure that I was registered for my upcoming classes.

I won't tell you it was easy. I had many crying nights, but while I was crying, I was submitting those papers. I kept a positive attitude towards school and my future endeavors, even though I was sitting in a dark room mourning the death of mom.

Many individuals go through similar and even more

extreme darkness in their lives, but with a positive mindset, you can beat all the odds. Ohio Congressman, Leslie Brown, is another great example of what maintaining a positive mindset can do. He first made a name for himself as a motivational speaker and has a signature phrase he uses when he speaks to a crowd. That phrase is, "It's possible." Brown will ask the crowd to think about what their personal and professional goals are, and then he will tell them to repeat the words, "It's possible."

The funny thing is, Brown did not always believe that good things were possible for him. Brown, his twin brother, and his three other siblings were all adopted, and Brown recalls that while his twin brother did well in school, he was labeled "educable mentally retarded" by the school system. He tells the story of one time when he went into a classroom to find someone, and the classroom teacher asked him to solve a problem on the board. He told the teacher he was not part of the class, but the teacher asked him to solve the problem anyway. When he said he couldn't, the teacher asked why not. Other kids in the class explained that he was the "dumb twin," and Brown agreed with them. That teacher walked right up to him and advised him never to accept anyone else's negative impression of him again, telling him, "Someone's opinion of you does not have to become your reality."

For Leslie Brown, that chance encounter, when he stepped into a classroom that was not even his own, was transformative. Of course, he still had a long journey ahead, but that short exchange with that teacher was one of the turning points that enabled Brown to begin to overcome negativity and start to think positively about his future potential. Brown describes feeling liberated by the incident.

When people think of positive thinking, many people

think back to the Methodist minister and motivational speaker, Norman Vincent Peale. Back in 1952, when Peale published the book "The Power of Positive Thinking," the book was widely criticized by academics for being too anecdotal and not supported by enough scientific evidence. But the advice Peale offered in his book must have struck a chord. The book went on to sell five million copies worldwide and was translated into 40 languages.

So what was Peale's message? He offered several steps to overcoming negativity. His first piece of advice to readers was that they should create a mental picture of their own success, and never doubt that mental image. This is very important hence the reason I had to call back my school counselor and tell him I wanted to start school now, not later, but now. I had created a mental picture of my success in my head, and I wasn't about to let anything get in my way.

Peale also warned readers that whenever a negative thought about their potential arose, they must deliberately cancel out that thought by thinking of something positive. I also used this piece of advice from Peale by starting to remember Mommy in a happy way rather than crying. I began to reminisce about the fun times we had, how vocal she was, and the many trips she made to my high school to ensure I was following the rules.

Peale went on to tell people not to build up the obstacles they face through fear. Instead, they should analyze all their obstacles and figure out ways around them. There were many other pieces of advice in the book, including the reminder that everyone else is probably just as scared deep down as you are, and no one can ever be you as well as you can.

To be positive in negative situations, you have to have hope. You have to be able to believe that you can create your own future. While we are all influenced by things that happened in our past, our past doesn't have to define our future. That is why professor, leadership coach, and author Marshall Goldsmith advocates providing "feedforward," rather than feedback.

"There is a fundamental problem with all types of feed-back," Goldsmith wrote. "It focuses on the past, on what has already occurred – not on the infinite variety of opportunities that can happen in the future. As such, feedback can be limited and static, as opposed to expansive and dynamic."

For years, Goldsmith has conducted a feedforward exercise with leaders and business executives. He asks participants to play two roles. In the first role, they must provide someone else with feedforward. In other words, they must give someone suggestions that will be helpful for the future. In the second role, they must accept feedforward by listening to someone else's suggestions for their future and learning as much as they can from it.

Most participants reported that, although providing feedback can sometimes be uncomfortable, providing feedforward is fun. Providing negative feedback can reinforce a feeling of failure and put people on the defensive. By contrast, when people are provided with feedforward, they tend not to take it personally. Feedforward reminds people that while they can't change the past, they can change the future. Goldsmith argues that feedforward is well-suited to successful people because to be successful, you need to be willing to look ahead and envision how things could be better. You also need to be prepared to accept advice that can help you improve.

In the preface to her book "Life Coaching for Successful Women," Valorie Burton, life coach, author, and founder of the Coaching and Positive Psychology Institute (CaPP), is quick to acknowledge her fears. She wrote that "A key to your success is developing a critical skill that every successful woman possesses in abundance: resilience. Successful women think differently in the face of fear, failure, setbacks, and challenges."

Burton believes that resilience is a skill that can be learned and constantly improved upon. She recognizes that everyone gets stuck from time to time, and suggests you can coach yourself out of situations that leave you feeling stuck by asking the right questions. For example, consider the relatively simple problem of procrastination. When you find yourself stuck procrastinating, you can ask yourself whether or not you are spending your time the way you want to. If the answer is no, you can follow up by asking yourself how you can refocus.

Developing resilience is an ongoing process, but it can be a necessary one on the path to success. Burton describes success as "harmony of purpose, resilience, and joy." These three elements are critical to success because everyone wants to have purpose and joy in their lives. However, when you find something that gives you purpose and brings you joy, you must find the resilience to hold on to that sense of purpose and defend it.

The obstacle of fear is actually an acronym for false evidence appearing real, the great Zig Ziglar once quipped. He pointed out that many people create worries that aren't really there. For example, some may worry about spending more time with their families when they are at work, and worry about spending more time at work when they are home. But, whether the obstacles you face are minor distractions, or more serious, soul crushing-setbacks, the answer to overcoming them involves setting goals and working towards them without fear.

By setting goals, you are establishing a target that gives you something to work toward. Having a goal helps you to be more efficient and hopeful. Therefore, make it a priority to always set goals because when faced with adverse situations, having set goals in place helps you to remain positive and optimistic about the future.

PART II

YOUR GOALS ARE WORTH FIGHTING FOR

CHAPTER THREE: CHOOSE FRIENDS THAT ALIGN WITH YOUR LIFE GOALS

❦

There is an often-quoted expression, "Show me your company, and I can tell you who you are." That expression is sometimes quoted as "Show me who your friends are, and I will show you your future." Either way, the message is clear. Your life path is influenced by the company you keep.

As life progresses, things change. Never allow anyone to let you feel guilty about making positive strides in your life, whether it be a change in friendship, relationship, or association. Many people are described as being ungrateful for merely changing relationships or friendships, but the fact is, as life progresses, we have to admit many people can remain in our hearts but not in our lives. Life is a cycle. There will be changes, and, as things change, you need to change. Changing associations or aligning yourselves with people who match your future endeavors does not necessarily mean forgetting anyone. All it does is put you in better alignment with your goals and with people with whom you share common interests. You are the captain of your ship. You know where you are headed and where your final destination should be. Do not allow anyone to sway you away from where you are headed. In Jamaican terms, my mom often used this quote "better you vex than me, but me naah loose." In simple terms, I'd rather you be upset; I'm not putting my future on hold to please anyone.

At first glance, it might sound strange to suggest choosing friends that align with your life goals. After all, we all have that one crazy friend, right? It is certainly ok to have a few friends who may be taking a different path from you. They are not necessarily the wrong friends to have. None of my friends are in the law enforcement field; we do not share common interests when it comes to careers, but we do share a lot of other similar goals and partnerships. My friends all have diverse careers while others are still working on getting themselves together, and that's totally fine because spice is the variety of life. The bigger issue is whether your friends support you as you pursue your dreams or steer you away from them.

As Howell Consultations puts it, "The right people around you can motivate you, encourage your happiness, and help you in various ways throughout your life, while the wrong friends can encourage feelings of helplessness, confusion, and low morality without us even realizing."

The problem, according to Howell Consultations, is that at some point in life, depending on our state of mind at the time, we can let people into our lives who might not have the best intentions, even for themselves. They might offer smiles and laughs that feel like friendship, but that camaraderie might be fake.

Howell Consultations advises three steps to choosing friends. First, be conscious of how people express themselves to you, how they treat you, how they speak of others, and how they treat others. Second, be mindful of the halo effect, which is defined as the tendency for an impression in one area to influence an opinion in another area. For example, your hairdresser may be good at what she does, she makes you feel pretty and satisfied every time she does your hair, but that does not necessarily mean she will be an honest, trustworthy, and loyal friend. Finally, choose your friends. As children, our parents may have chosen our friends for us, but later in life, we have to be careful not to fall into the habit of letting others make choices for us. You are the one experiencing your life, and you should do it on your terms. Your friends' friends are not your friends. Choose your friends.

In his famous book, "How to Win Friends and Influence People," Dale Carnegie devotes an entire chapter to the need that people have to feel important. But he wrote that chapter not only to illustrate the positive effect of making someone feel important, but also to warn about the lengths that some people will go to make themselves feel important even if it means using you and only showing up when it is beneficial to them.

For example, he tells the story of a woman who took to her bed for about ten years. During that time, her older mother walked to the third floor multiple times a day, carrying meals and other items of comfort. At some point, the woman's weary older mother passed away. When the mother died, the woman got up and went on with living her life. Clearly, the way that this mother and daughter were interacting was not healthy for either of them. It was clear that only the daughter was gaining. Perhaps she was unwittingly taking advantage of her mother because she wasn't willing to face her problems or fears. Maybe there were other dynamics in play that made the daughter feel dependent. Whatever the case, the message was not that they should have ended their relationship; after all, they were mother and daughter and loved each other. But their relationship could have improved if they had stepped back and assessed how they were treating each other, and whether they were serving as support for each other.

Sometimes, it is necessary for friends or family members to examine the relationships they have with each other and evaluate whether they are really growing together, or whether the relationship is progressing in a way that is unproductive or beneficial to only one party. If it is not productive, it is up to you to choose to make a change, whether that means handling the relationship differently or creating some distance that will allow you to grow. Whatever decision you make, it should be beneficial to both of you. Don't let anyone use you to their advantage; people can be deceving.

What makes a good friend? Shasta Nelson, an author, and speaker who has written three books on the subject of friendship, points out that in this day and age where social media is so prevalent, many of us know more people than ever before, but may still feel lonely and unsure of who we can confide in.

According to Nelson, "Our social networks keep growing and growing and growing, but we still have doubts about whether we actually have a safety net and who should be in it." She further went on to elaborate that the three pillars of friendship are positivity, consistency, and vulnerability. As she explains it, positivity is because we all want to feel loved, consistency is because we can only feel loved if we feel known, and vulnerability is critical, because we can only feel known if we can share ourselves.

We may know a lot of positive people who we like, but friendship isn't only about liking people. Nelson states that to truly know a friend, we have to have the consistency of having spent time with that person to develop that friend-ship. Consistency is the history we build over time. Vulnera-bility is where we share and let people in. Nelson points out that vulnerability doesn't have to mean sharing skeletons in your closet; it can mean sharing your hopes and dreams or your fears. Never get caught up with the belief that you have to share your personal business with your friends. That's your decision to make based on your assessment of the type of friends you have. Friends serve different purposes; some you can confide in, others you can't.

Choosing friends who align with your life goals is not as much about choosing friends based on what they do, but it is about choosing friends with whom you can build histories and share your goals, and friends who will support you as you pursue those goals. It is important to invest in strong friendships, but having too many social media connections that are just acquaintances rather than friends may increase stress, according to mental strength trainer and author, Amy Morin. In an article in Forbes magazine, Morin noted that a University of Edinburgh Business School study showed that people with too many social media contacts were often preoccupied with presenting the ideal image of themselves to their online contacts. The stress was particularly acute when people were trying too hard to look cool for one set of contacts, when this would be less appropriate for another.

But, beyond the issues of social media, Morin also noted that several studies have shown that genuine positive friendships can boost someone's personal and professional success. For example, she noted that a psychological study, published in the April 2013 issue of Psychological Science, showed that when we go through periods of low self-control, we seek out people who are self-disciplined. In other words, having disciplined friends might help motivate us and put us back on track when we are going through rough times. Also, having strong connections to the right people might give us a reason to pause before making reckless decisions. Our friends should be our support, and they can also serve as our role models. If we have friends who we respect and look up to, we might think twice before making decisions that might disappoint them.

Entrepreneur Candice Galek, who founded the company BikiniLuxe, believes it is ironic that while we may be picky about who we date, we often hang around a group of friends who we happen to know out of habit, without giving it much thought. This can be problematic, and friendships should be evaluated with care. If you know someone who is extremely selfish and always leaves you feeling bad, that might be a relationship you need to avoid. If you feel you are restricted to only talking about the past with old friends, Galek advises considering reducing visits with those friends, but not necessarily eliminating them. A friendship with longevity is often something worth preserving, but don't develop the habit of holding on to just memories or saving face. If the friendship is not working out or is unhealthy, move on.

While you might not want friends exclusively in your field of work, Galek notes that having work-related friendships can be fruitful. Not only are you likely to have a common interest, but friends in your area of work can provide career advice or serve as sounding boards when you face difficult work-related dilemmas. They can also be valuable contacts who might be able to help with references or work-related introductions you might need down the road. Of course, if you develop friends you meet through work, you can't only think of them in terms of their value as work contacts. If these are real friendships, based on honesty and respect, they should be as valuable to you personally as professionally.

While in school, we tend to form friendships with people our own age. As adults, Galek says that it is important and valuable to have friendships of all ages. Older friends may share wisdom and experience that can help as we make life choices, but younger friends can renew us through energy and exuberance.

Ranked as one of the top hospitals in the USA, the Mayo Clinic has specialties across a wide range of areas. According to the clinic, adults with strong friendships and social support have reduced risks of depression, high blood pressure, and unhealthy body mass index. Friends can increase someone's sense of belonging and purpose, boost happiness, reduce stress, improve self-confidence, help in coping with trauma, and encourage positive life changes and healthy lifestyles. Developing and maintaining healthy friendships involves give-and-take, and the Mayo Clinic advises that we think of friendship as an emotional bank account. Every act of kindness is a deposit, while negativity draws down the account. The clinic has several other recommendations for building successful relationships, such as paying attention to friends through listening, eye-contact, and observing body language. We should open up and share with friends, to show them that we trust them with special concerns. This deepens connections and builds intimacy. Being responsible, reliable, and dependable is also key, and that includes demonstrating that you can keep confidences private. Building relationships also means making an effort to check in with friends and schedule time to see them or speak to them.

No doubt, having the right people around you and investing in the right friendships can be beneficial to your life. But having the wrong people in your circle can create long term depression and cause many losses. Many people claim they do know the definition of being a loyal friend and play the role for years. But the moment the sun stops shining on your doorstep, they completely forget about the friendship. Choose wisely, friends can make you, and they can break you.

CHAPTER FOUR: TAKE ACTION AND BOOST YOUR "NETWORTH"

B oosting your "networth" is about bringing it all together. That means defining your goals, really examining what you are passionate about, and being willing to chase your dreams. It means examining what your strengths are and whether you are using them. It means considering whether you are feeling fulfilled in your current situation.

Taking action begins with evaluating what your goals are and the steps you need to take to achieve them. Consider what would make you feel happy and successful. Think about how you can shine. Then make a plan and stick to it. Stick to it through pain; stick to it through pleasure; stick to it no matter the circumstances - just stick to it.

You will undoubtedly encounter obstacles on the way, but you have to will yourself past them. Envision the success that you want to achieve and put thoughts about failure out of your mind. When you encounter a roadblock, do not let it stop you. Analyze it. Coach yourself about why you will not let this stop you. Consider alternative routes, but do not let yourself be crippled by fear.

It is through your toughest time that you will realize the importance of surrounding yourself with people who will help you, and people who will encourage you and cheer you on. Do not listen to naysayers who are trying to lead you off the path. You know in your heart who your true friends are. Trust them. But, most importantly, trust yourself.

Once you have a plan, how do you begin pursuing it? One of the first steps is to get organized. The author, speaker, and pastor, John C. Maxwell, has noted that people often talk about time management, but in reality, time can't be managed. Time is out of our control, but what we can control is our priorities.

"We need to determine how we will spend the twenty-four hours that we are blessed with every day. That requires prioritizing our time so we can get more production out of those hours," he wrote in his book, "Developing the Leader Within You."

Admittedly, with the pressures of modern life, it can be difficult to manage priorities. Maxwell warns that most people overestimate the importance of most things. One of the first steps of managing priorities, according to Maxwell, is learning how to overlook trivial tasks that can steal much of our time. In fact, when small problems are given too much attention, more significant problems can arise. He advises that chasing dreams means staying focused, so that small problems don't put your main priorities out of reach. Many people can find themselves paralyzed by the number of different tasks they have to deal with. Lion tamers at the circus would often carry a stool as they walked into a lion cage. According to Maxwell, the reason for that was that the lions would get confused, looking at the four legs of the stools trying to figure out which one to focus on, and that would make them easier to tame. The point is we can all get confused by multiple priorities and responsibilities, and that makes it harder to focus on any one thing. Managing your schedule means seriously considering what is most important to do, and planning the right time to do it and how to get it done. It may mean assigning scores to different priorities so that you can organize them in order of importance. A daily planner would be useful in this regard to prioritize your day-to-day activities, and making an annual vision board is terrific for tracking your long-term goals.

Maxwell also cautions that part of prioritization means making sure that you continue to live a healthy life as you pursue your dreams. For example, we all have busy periods, but Maxwell warns that if there is less than 20 percent white space in your calendar on a regular basis, you may risk overwhelming yourself to a breaking point. Organizing your priorities includes taking care of yourself.

After prioritizing, the next step is forming a positive mental attitude. Author Napoleon Hill, in his book, "You Can Work Your Own Miracles" defines a positive mental attitude as, "the habit of choosing a definite goal and marching forward toward its attainment without hesitations because of either commendation or condemnation."

But Hill also recognizes that there are other aspects to having a positive mental attitude, such as mastering your emotions. This involves facing the pleasant and unpleasant things that affect your life while trying to keep a cool head. It also means looking for good qualities in others, and at the same time, being prepared to find bad qualities without being shocked. Hill believes that a positive mental attitude affects not only how you focus and perceive yourself; it also affects how others perceive you. For example, Hill believes that the mental attitude of public speakers can have more impact on how their speeches are interpreted than the actual words in their speeches.

To form a positive mental attitude, Hill recommends

associating with people who are inspiring, and engaging in healthy and creative projects, while trying to avoid negative-minded people. He also suggests conditioning yourself to continually focus on the positives, until looking on the bright side starts to become automatic when you face challenges. Finally, forming a positive attitude involves accepting that you have the power to control how you look at situations.

Training yourself to have a positive mental attitude can be challenging, but the upside is that it is possible for anyone. As Hill puts it, "the most profound fact regarding a positive mental attitude is that everyone has the privilege of adopting it and using it for all purposes, without money and without price."

If it seems difficult to form and maintain a positive mental attitude, life-coach, author, and public speaker, Tony Robbins suggests considering for a moment how easy it is to discourage yourself. Think of how quickly something can put you in a bad mood. Think of how a bit of unexpected criticism can make you feel self-doubt. If you can discourage yourself that easily or get in a bad mood so quickly, you have the power to encourage yourself that quickly as well. In his book "Awaken the Giant Within," Robbins acknowledges that pain and discouragement are powerful forces, but he suggests you might be able to use them to your advantage. For example, if you want to try a new way of doing something, maybe you can begin to focus on the pain of the old way of doing it. You can also harness the power of pain by focusing on what you will miss out on if you don't make the changes you want to make.

"The greatest leverage you can create for yourself is the pain that comes from inside, not outside," Robbins wrote. "Knowing that you have failed to live up to your own standards for your life is the ultimate pain."

Of course, Robbins warns, pain can't be the only emotion

that governs your actions. You must also remind yourself what you want and why you want it. Why will this new venture make you happy? What other things might you accomplish if you set yourself on a new path? The more positive reasons you give yourself to make a change, and make it soon, the more motivation you will have.

I found inspiration to make a change from banking to law enforcement because of the positive attitude the police officers tended to display whenever they visited my community. They were very respectful but also stern. By having a good mental attitude about the police department, I began to internalize some of the qualities that I have that would make me suitable for the department. Working in banking was ok, but I felt like an outsider because my heart was not into it. I put on a bright smile every day to serve the customers, but when I got home at night, I would be telling my mother how unhappy I was. She encouraged me to stay, but I just couldn't. I had to do what was best for me and what would make me happy. Many people thought that me joining the police department was somewhat impossible since I was the first person from my family to be a police officer. But I don't settle on my Ls; I turn all my can'ts into cans because it is possible once you believe in yourself.

What is important to remember is that not everyone figures out their dreams when they are in high school or college. Some people have a dream from when they are very young, and others don't find their calling until later. Julia McWilliams had initially planned to become a writer. She submitted short stories to the New Yorker, but none of them were published. Julia eventually lost interest in that idea and worked for a while in the advertising department of a furniture store. She later got a job working for the government, and while working for the government, she met and married a coworker, Paul Child. When her husband was transferred through work to France, Julia decided to take a cooking course. She was thirty-six, and while she had always loved food, she had never really known much about cooking before. Once she learned how to cook, though, she was immediately hooked. Julia Child went on to share her passion for cooking with the world through cookbooks and cooking shows. Cooking was a passion she discovered later in life, but Julia Child is remembered as one of the iconic personalities of the cooking world. One of her favorite rules she used to have about cooking also applies to life, "The only real stumbling block is fear of failure."

Investor and entrepreneur, Ray Dalio, has found that what guided him most on his path to success were his principles. In his book, "Principles: Life and Work," Dalio defines principles as your personal set of rules for life that you may develop through experience, or reflection, or based on ideas you were taught at some point. You should form your principles with "humility and open-mindedness," Dalio says; you want to live by your own beliefs, but still consider the best ideas and advice available to you. Dalio feels your principles are personal, and you have to develop them for yourself. But, while your principles must be unique to you, it's not necessarily wrong to adopt some of your principles from someone else. After all, we probably have similar principles with like-minded people. If you adopt someone else's principles without really thinking about them and internalizing them, however, the rules that you try to live by might be inconsistent with your nature.

For example, one of Dalio's ideals is to "strive for a lot and fail well." By that, he means he likes to take chances, even if that means experiencing some failures that can be personal learning opportunities. However, Dalio spent his career in the finance industry, where there are cycles of ups and downs, and where a certain amount of risk-taking is built into the process. People who work in less volatile industries or who are more cautious by nature might have different principles.

Whatever your temperament or personal philosophy may be, Dalio thinks it is critical to codify for yourself a set of principles to live by. He writes, "Having a good set of principles is like having a good collection of recipes for success. All successful people operate by principles that help them be successful, though what they choose to be successful at varies enormously, so their principles vary."

Many people who chase their dreams face some challenges in making them happen. Russell H. Conwell was a Baptist minister who is remembered for being the founder and first president of Temple University. In his 1917 collection of essays called "Increasing Personal Efficiency," Conwell pointed out that while obstacles are to be expected, anything earned by sacrifice and "downright hard work" is priceless. The reason for that is twofold. When you work hard at something, not only do you gain a great sense of accomplishment, but you become more expert at what you are trying to do with the more work you put in.

As Conwell puts it, "The greater the difficulty surmounted, the more you will value your achievement and the greater power you will have to keep on working even after you have reached your goal."

After you have identified your goal and formulated a plan to reach it, the next most important thing to do is to just get to it. Entrepreneur Daymond John notes in his book "Rise and Grind" that the first step doesn't have to be a big one. John defines the "grind" in the title of his book by this simple progression: act, learn, repeat. He notes that if you take just one step and it works out well, it could be luck, but if you can do it over and over again, and you can keep taking steps forward, then you are onto something. He calls it a "keep moving" mentality. If you demand excellence in what you put out, he says, you might find it in what you get back.

John recalls that when his company FUBU was first getting started, he and his colleagues came back from their first trade show in Las Vegas with hundreds of thousands of dollars in orders, but they still couldn't get a bank loan. It was frustrating, but they understood that chasing a dream was about showing resilience in the face of setbacks. In the end, John felt the path to success was about finding the desire, drive, and determination to keep grinding through.

Life has a way of throwing bricks at us, but it is imperative that you be resilient and believe in yourself. Even if no one else supports you, support yourself. Always remember, time lost cannot be regained. It doesn't matter what we do or where we go; time will pass regardless, so practice to make the best use of it. Try to build and maintain a growth mindset throughout all adversities because all challenges are still an opportunity to rise, once we have life.

www.ingramcontent.com/pod-product-compliance
Lightning Source LLC
Chambersburg PA
CBHW051740040426
42447CB00008B/1236